Cycles of Nature

Hibernation

by Jaclyn Jaycox

raintree
a Capstone company — publishers for children

Raintree is an imprint of Capstone Global Library Limited, a company incorporated in England and Wales having its registered office at 264 Banbury Road, Oxford, OX2 7DY – Registered company number: 6695582

www.raintree.co.uk
myorders@raintree.co.uk

Editor: Alesha Sullivan
Designer: Charmaine Whitman
Media Researcher: Morgan Walters
Production Specialist: Katy LaVigne

ISBN 978 1 4747 9514 2 (hardback)
ISBN 978 1 4747 9526 5 (paperback)

British Library Cataloguing in Publication Data
A full catalogue record for this book is available from the British Library.

Acknowledgements
Alamy: imageBROKER, 15; Shutterstock: A3pfamily, 21, BGSmith, 11, Coatesy, (hedge hog) Cover, 13, Dmitri Gomon, 9, Greg and Jan Ritchie, (bear) Cover, Jukka Jantunen, 7, Kletr, 19, McoBra89, 17, Ondrej Prosicky, (bat) Cover, Real PIX, 5, Toluk, (circles) design element throughout

Every effort has been made to contact copyright holders of material reproduced in this book. Any omissions will be rectified in subsequent printings if notice is given to the publisher.

All the internet addresses (URLs) given in this book were valid at the time of going to press. However, due to the dynamic nature of the internet, some addresses may have changed, or sites may have changed or ceased to exist since publication. While the author and publisher regret any inconvenience this may cause readers, no responsibility for any such changes can be accepted by either the author or the publisher.

Printed in India
983

Contents

A long nap

When the winter comes, it is time for some animals to sleep. When they wake up, it will be spring! This long sleep is called hibernation.

A bat hibernating

A deep sleep

Hibernation is a special kind
of sleep. Winters can be very cold.
Food can be hard to find.
Some animals live through the
cold by hibernating.

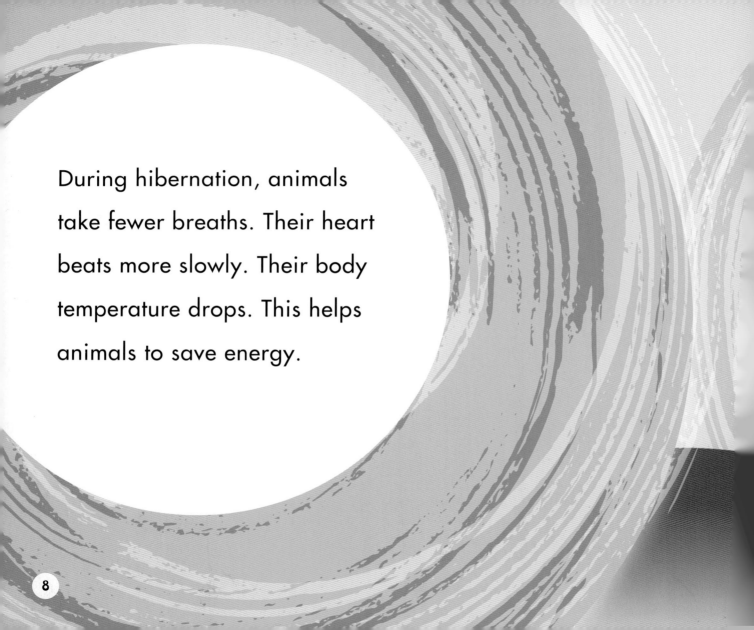

During hibernation, animals take fewer breaths. Their heart beats more slowly. Their body temperature drops. This helps animals to save energy.

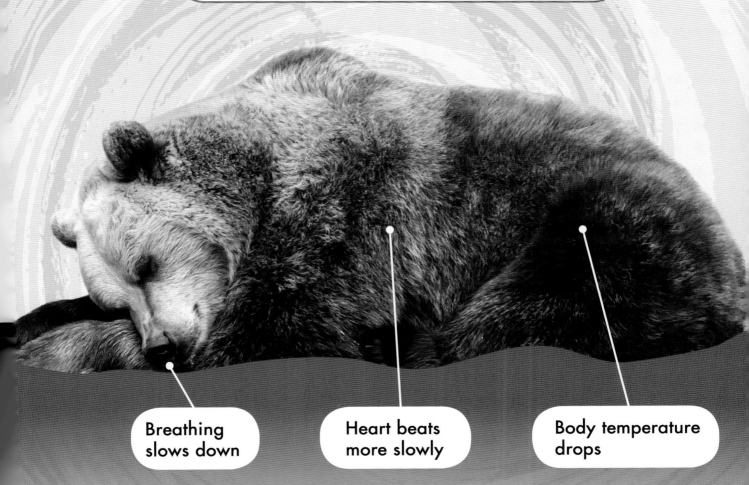

Body changes during hibernation

Breathing slows down

Heart beats more slowly

Body temperature drops

Eat, eat, eat

Animals eat lots of food before hibernating. They store food as fat. The fat is used as energy while they sleep. It also keeps them warm.

Sleepy creatures

Many animals hibernate
when it is cold. Bears sleep
all winter long. They curl up
in dens. Bats sleep in caves.
Hedgehogs snooze in nests.

Hedgehog

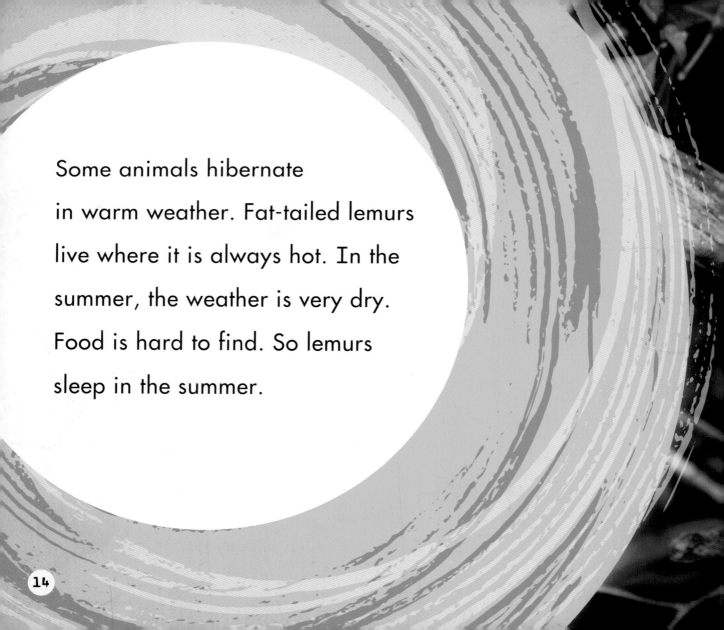

Some animals hibernate
in warm weather. Fat-tailed lemurs
live where it is always hot. In the
summer, the weather is very dry.
Food is hard to find. So lemurs
sleep in the summer.

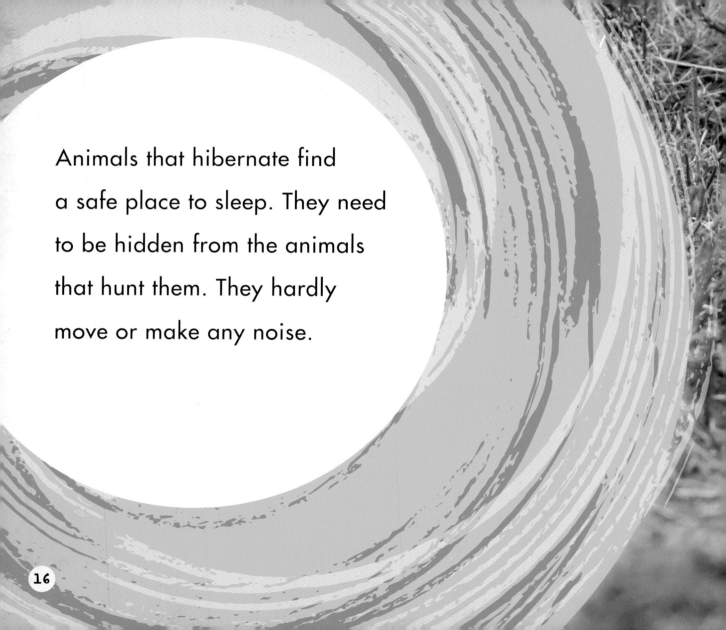

Animals that hibernate find a safe place to sleep. They need to be hidden from the animals that hunt them. They hardly move or make any noise.

Marmot in a den

Hibernation problems

Smoke from burning things
pollutes the air. People cut down
trees. These things cause the
weather to change. The Earth
is getting warmer.

These climate changes make it hard for some animals to hibernate. People can help the planet and the seasons. We can plant more trees. We can keep the air cleaner.

Glossary

den a place where a wild animal lives; a den may be a hole in the ground or a trunk of a tree

energy the strength to do active things without getting tired

hibernate to spend winter in a deep sleep; animals hibernate to survive harsh temperatures and lack of food

pollute to make something dirty or unsafe

season one of the four parts of the year; winter, spring, summer and autumn are seasons

temperature how hot or cold something is

weather the condition outdoors at a certain time and place; weather changes with each season

Find out more

All About Animals in Winter (Celebrate Winter), Martha E. Rustad (Raintree, 2017)

Hibernation (Animal Adaptations), Pamela McDowell (AV2 by Weigl, 2016)

Sleep, Bear! (National Geographic Readers), Shelby Alinsky (National Geographic, 2015)

Websites

Fun Hibernation Facts
www.scholastic.com/teachers/articles/teaching-content/fun-hibernation-facts/

Hibernation Facts for Kids
www.coolfactsforkids.com/hibernation-facts-for-kids/

How the Changing Seasons Affect Hedgehogs: Video Clip
www.bbc.co.uk/bitesize/clips/z7kc87h

Comprehension questions

1. How else do you think Earth's warming temperatures could affect animals?

2. What do you think could happen if an animal doesn't eat enough before hibernating?

Index